W9-AUM-186

PAMUKKALE

"HIERAPOLIS"

TEVHİT KEKEÇ
ARCHAEOLOG,
RESEARCHER OF THE BERGAMA MUSEUM

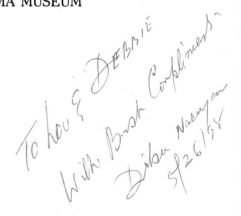

HİTİT COLOR
KARTPOSTAL SANAYİ TİCARET VE PAZARLAMA LİMİTED ŞİRKETİ
Cağaloğlu Yokuşu, Çele Han No. 39 İstanbul Tel: 526 56 51 - 520 78 49

Art Selection and Design:
Melih Öndün

Illustration:
Melek Öndün

Photographs:
Hitit Color

Translation:
Çağlayan Somer

Typesetting:
Patrol Ajans

All Rights Reserved.
The contents of this book, whether verbal or pictoral,
may not be published in whole or in part without the
permission of publisher.

Hitit Color 1997 İSTANBUL
ISBN 975-7487-00-7

Cover: The Travertines at Sunset.

CONTENTS

Preface

In today's Turkey where Tourism is increasing a lot in importance, there is a special interest in books and guides which take the enthusiastic travellers closer to historical cities and antique ruins.

Thus, it pleases me very much that Mr. **Tevhit Kekeç** with whom I have been in close contact for many years due to our Pergamon cooperation, has undertaken to write a guide through Hierapolis-Pamukkale.

I wish the booklet a lot of success.

Dr. Wolfgang Radt
Leader of the Pergamon Excavations.

ITS GEOGRAPHY
AND HISTORY

Hierapolis is seventeen kilometers to the north of Denizli and it is 1840 m high. This height is 100-150 m above Lycos plains and 360 m above the sea. It came into existance through geologically broken and scattered-around earth layers. On the 3rd km of the Denizli, Burdur, Afyonkarahisar highway there is a turning to the north. This road which is 11 km long leads to Pamukkale. On the other hand, a train can be taken up to Yoncalı and by following the same road Pamukkale can be reached. In the antique times it was inhabited by the natives, the Luvis (1900 B.C.) Between the years 550-500 B.C. there was a city called Idrara or (Kıdrara). This was the most civilised city of the Lycos valley. The people of this city, who were called Hydraleitar, ruled over wide lands including Manisa in the north, Collosia in the east and Laodıca in the south. As Hydrala started to lose its importance with time, people started to gather around Hieron and they built a temple there. In the second century B.C., King Attalos 11., the king of Pergamon, built a new city in place of this holy town after winning a war against the Seleykos. This city was named after Hiera, the wife of the Mysian king and founder of Pergamon. Thus the city Hierapolis was also called he "Holy City." The oldest inscription belonging to this city is an order, written in the honor of Apollonis, the mother of Eumenis.

Being on the earthquake zone, the city came down with various earthquakes, but was rebuilt. In 133 B.C. Pergamon was dirctly connected to Rome after the will of King Attalos 111. and like all the other small cities connected to this kingdom, Hierapolis got connected to Rome.

The city, which was destroyed by an earthquake in 17 A.D. during the reing of Tiberius and then again in 60 A.D. during the reing of Nero, was rebuilt again. And it gained a lot of importance because of its spas and mineral waters during the reign of Hadrianus and Caracalla, and it underwent a lot of construction's again. The remnants seen today are the remnants of Roman construction.

Christianity started to spread in this region in 40 A.D. In 87 A.D. St.Phillip, who was one of the twelve apostles, was killed in Hierapolis. And a church was built there in the name of St.Phillip. The city played an important role in the Spreading of Christianity in Little Asia. As the Roman civilization became larger between 96 and 192 A.D., Hierapolis was again reconstructed and lived its most brilliant periods during the reigns of Antonius Plus (138-161 A.D.), Septimus Severus (193-198 A.D.), and his son Caracalla (211-217 A.D.).

During this time Hierapolis was called the leader of the east. When Rome was divided into two in 395 A.D. the city went under the reign of Byzantine. Hierapolis, which showed great development in the second and third centuries, continued this development under the Byzantine reign, especially during the times of Constatine the Great who made Hierapolis the capital of some parts of the Phrygia region. And it also became the center of Bishopric. Hierapolis gradually became less and less important. And during this period no architectural piece was added, and even

Antique theater of Laodicea

Remnants of St. Philip Martyrion

the old ones could not be saved properly. The city continued this state until the eleventh century. In 1071 after winning the Malazgirt War, the Seljuks, little by little, started to take over Anatolia, and, eventually, they captured the city Laodicia in 1094. And they began to live in the Lycos valley. The cities of Laodicia, Hierapolis and Tropolis, that used to be rivals before the Turks, took over got together in order to defend themselves against the Turks. But this pact did not prevent the Turks from advancing. And armies under the command of Mehmet and Server Gazi captured Colossi and Laodicia. This war was ended in 1097 after the Turkish commanders were killed in the fight. After the negotiations with the Byzantine and the Turks, Laodicia was given to the Turks as war indemnity. At those times Laodica had become an unimportant and disordered city. Although Laodica was out of the reign of the Turks because Seljuk ruler Kılıçarslan I lost a fight against the Crusades, after a short while, it again came under the reign of the Turks.

In 1119 the Byzantine Emperor Juanis, took Laodica back, but the city had become a battle field between the Byzantine and the Turks. And this situation lasted until the Latin Empire was built.

The Latin Emperor Theodor Laskaris took all of the small governors and their lands under his reign. The city was taken back by Gıyaseddin Keyhüsrev (1192-1194, 1204-1210) in 1210, and all of the

Pamukkale village

Menderes Valley was taken over. Later on, the Menderes River was accepted as a border as a result of negotiations of Turks and Byzantine.

During the reign of Izzeddin Keykavus (1246-1248, 1249-1261) the Mongolian pressure increased and the ruler gave Laodica back, in order to be able to get some help from Byzantine (1258). But this reign did not last long. All of the Lycos Valley, except for Tropolis, came under the reign of the Turks again. During the reign of Gıyaseddin Keyhusrev, (1266-1283) the two sons of the Seljukian Vizier were presented by the Ilhanians with Laodicia and Colossa, and these two cities were ruled by the two sons of the Vizier Sahip Ata. Their names were Taceddin Hüseyin and Nasrettin Hasan. After them the cities went to the Germiyan Principality and it many times changed hands between these two principalities.

Thus, in this way Ladicia and Hierapolis went under the reign of the Inanç Principality in the thirteenth century, and eventually Hierapolis went under the reign of the Turks under the reign of the Denizli Commander. These cities, which grew very weak as a result of many many wars, were completely destroyed by earthquakes and were deserted by the inhabitants. The life process of these antique cites was thus completed.

Frontinus (Domitian) door consisting of two towers and three arches

THE WATERS OF PAMUKKALE (HIERAPOLIS)

This wonderful place has come about by the waters leaving its dregs on a platform- which is 150 m. higher than the Lycos valley which is to the north of Denizli and which is approximately 4 km on the south skirts of the Salpak Mountains-and forming hills there.

At the same time it being closed to the tough and cold air currents emphasizes the importance of the mineral waters. The famous travertines are caused by the waters which are a mixture of carbondioxide (CO_2) and calcium (Ca) running down the southern flanks.

Many mineral springs which are connected to the big fault at the Büyük Menderes Valley, are hot underground waters which come from far places. In this flat place where earlier Hierapolis used to be there were many hot water springs at different temperatures. Other then the big main spring which is now being run by a motel, (in the swimming pool of this motel there are antique columns) there is another one which sprang open in the earthquake in the nineteenth century. The temperature of both springs is about 35°C. These hot waters were very important in the antique city and through ancient sources we learn that there also was a cult of Heracles, the God of health and hot waters.

Because there are Carbondioxide compounds in the composition of the water, the water comes up above the ground, and as a result of this, the calcer, which would get seperated from the Carbondioxide gas, precipitates to the ground, and forms white layers and dregs on the soil. These travertines, which are white, gradually get darker due to contact with air. That is why the waters have to run constantly. The very dark parts are the areas where teh waters don't flow regularly.

But then again the flowing of the water in the form of small cascades has helped nature to form fine high - relief and figures of such high art that even the work of the most talented master cannot be compared to.

A view from the travertine formations.

To see these natural figures, to watch the playful water and the sun in the small lakes on the terraces, to appreciate travertines whilst walking up to the remnants from the Ecirli Village, and taking a look at the green and wide valley after reaching the top, is something that gives us infinite pleasure.

To see the settling of the elements in the water is enough to make a small experiment. First, some soil, a bottle, a broom, and an earthen pitcher are put under the cascades; then, after waiting for two days, it can be seen that these have turned totally white. Plus, the water of Pamukkale is clear, drinkable, soft and a little bitterish.

Pamukkale Water

The analysis measures and the composition:

CATIONS		MILIGRAMS
Potassium Chloride	"K"	23.5
Sodium Chloride	"Na"	32.5
Calcium Chloride	"Ca"	464.5
Magnesium Chlor.	"Mg"	91.1
Iron Chloride	"Fe"	0.036
Aluminium Chlor.	"Al"	2.34

ANIONS		MILIGRAMS
Chloride	"Cl"	53.00
Nitrate	"NO_3"	very little
Sulphate	"SO_4"	675.5
Nitrophosphate	"HPO_4"	1.08
Hydrocarbon	"HCO_3"	1045.3
		1774.88
Metasilicate Acid	"H_2S_{13}"	18.0
Carbondioxide	"CO_2"	1144.0
Reaction		6.0

The road leading to Hierapolis plateau from the Menderes Valley (up left)
The pool with columnes (down left)
Bottles covered with limestone completely (up)
Karahayıt. Red water having rich Ferrooxide

As can be seen from this analysis chart, the most common element found in water is Carbondioxide and dissolved Calcium.

This is the reason of the white layers and the travertines. The waters, which include Aluminum and sulfur in the composition, are especially good for the health. So, these spas are frequently visited because of this. These spas are most frequent around the Menderes Valley near Denizli. The impact of these spas have been most important in the foundation of Hierapolis. Even today, these spas, other than the travertines and the antique remnants, are the most important factor, which emphasize the importance of Pamukkale. As a result, these waters made the city an important cure and health center with its many public and private baths. Many people from all overthe world, who wished to get some rest, who wished to find a remedy for their illnesses, and also the ones who wished to spend some good time, came to Hierapolis. This water has been good for coroner diseases, high blood pressure and arteriosclerosis. In parallel, same as the Pergamon Asklepion, where emotional illnesses were treated by inculcation, patients here were treated with water.

Sunset beyond the travertines

Another speciality of this water is, that it cures skin diseases, especially allergic cases, and it is also good in strengthening and curing the eye muscles. The clergy in he antique times, by the help of this water, used to create miracles. Many temples were built in order to treat people, and the priests would take care of their patients in these temples. The patient would first be inculcated, ant then they would undergo a diet.

After that, they were taken to the Plutonium, and lader they would take long baths. And among all these things the only real remedy was naturally the long baths.

There were many people who suffered rheumatism, and could walk by walking sticks, and left in a perfeetly good shape. Not only ill people would come to the spas. Counsils, kings and philosophers too, would visit Hierapolis to have fun and to entertain themselves. The water has had many impacts on the city: The amount of visitors, getting wealthier, the increase in population, and the development of the city it self through an increase of beautiful architectural pieces. The numerous motels and spas which have been trying to serve many sick people is a very good example to the above mentioned situation.

RELIGION, DEMONS HOLE (Plutonium) AND THE HIERAPOLITAN FESTIVALS

Eventhough Zeus was the main god worshipped in Laodicia, in Hierapolis Apollo was worshipped as the ultimate God, and his cult had a very big importance. Other than the Apollo Cult, Goddess Leto was also worshipped. Her cult was a steep cave which was located 3 kms to the south of the Mondane (Akçeşme) village, and 9 kms to the north-west of Hierapolis. On the walls of this cave there are some inscriptions. One of these inscriptions tells that a vow was made by Flavianus Meneznes. According to Pavzanias, this Goddess was the protector of the mountains. Other than the Hierapolitans, the people of Dionysopolis would also worship Leto. She took her place in the mountains in order not to be disturbed by people. Her symbols were forest animals like the lion or a male deer. The cult of Heracles, the God of the healing water, was also in Hierapolis. According to these people's belief, a goddess was superior to a God. This situation also made women the head of the family.

According to "Nicatas", a famous historian from Collosai (Honaz), a poisonous snake called "Viper" was also worshipped. This same worshipping could also be seen in Leodicia. The Hierapolitan priests considered themselves immune to the toxic gases of the Plutonium. They used to live alonle because according to their belief, the more a man was distant to women the closer he was to God. In Hierapolis there was also a brotherhood sech which reminds us of the Ahi sect of the eastern civilizations. These hospitable people who had their own original signs would worship God Apollo.

This place, of which the source is on the south-west of the antique theater, was a means of making money for priests. It is a cave that produces Carbondioxide (CO_2). This place, which is situated in the city, was first called "Plutonium" (small volcanoe), later the name was changed into "Demon's hole" by the inhabitants. These suffocating gases helped the "Kybele" priests to make the people believe that they possessed supernatural powers.

According to the mythology, Kybele, the daughter of the skies and the first goddess of Anatolia, had a cult in Phyrigia as well. The priests of this goddess knew how to

Backside of the Apollon Temple. Architectural remnants (left)

27

take advantage from this toxicating gas of the cave. The animals, especially the birds, that came close to the cave would die in a short while, as a result of suffocation. The priests would enter this cave in great concentration and would stay in there without breathing. Their coming out alive of this cave would make people believe that they were superior and regarded this as a miracle. The priests would increase their superiority effect by claiming that they would contact with orcus in the caue, (1) who represented the death in the cave, and his demons. Patients suffering rheumatism were treated by these priests. Other than what Strabon tells us about the Plutonium, we also have information given by W.M. Ramsey in his book Phyrigia, published in 1897.

The waters of Hierapolis contain a lot of lime, but the most lime is in the hot springs. We can observe that any small flowing water makes its canals by limestone. In the south of the city the waters, running 100 feet above, look like frozen cascades. These cascades look like white fortresses, and thus comes the name Pamukkale (Cotton Fortress).

Another thing other than this is the hole called Plutonion-Chronion which is big enough for a person to enter in. Ando out of this hole a gas called "Mephitie" would come out, and it was called "the land of death." This hole is lost in the fourth century B.C.

This hole astonished the people in the antique times very much as well. Strabon says that if any living thing would come close to it, it would die. This place was situated in the southwest of the antique theater and to the north of the Holy Spring, which is now within the boundaries of the Turizm Motel. Today the hole, that produces toxic gas and which is called "Demon's Hole" amongst the natives, is covered with stone. The healing effect of the famos Hierapolis waters was attributed to gods. So the city acquired a holy

The relief showing Hierapolis Races on the wall of
the orchestra place of the Hierapolis Theater (up)
Camel wrestling was another part of the Hierapolis
festivales that was given particular interest (down)

characteristic because of the temples and
churches built. Ancient resources tell us
that, the city lived many brilliant and rich
eras since antique times because of this
precious water. Another quality of the
Pamukkale water is that it cleans dirt,
bleaches wool and fixes the color of dyes.
Wool, which has been dyed in alizarin,
turns to purple after being washed in this
water. Other than being a religious center,
Hierapolis was also an entertainment
center. And, among all the entertainments,
festivals occupy a special place. These
festivals, which were usually held in the
honor of Apollo, included various games,
athletic contests an musical entertainment.

The organization of these festivals was
made by the wealthy people of the city. The
festival manager was responsible of

Cavea of the Hierapolis Theater

training and educating the artists, players, athletes and musicians, and preparing them for the festival. The people who wanted to watch the festival had to pay money (silver) in order to be able to do so. The festival was managed by a comittee of six people, and among them the richest man of the city was the president of the committee. These festivals were attented by many spectators and contestants from all over Anatolia and even from Rome. The winners of the races and contests were presented with medals, money and various gifts. Other than these, their portraits would be printed on coins. Their big busts would be placed in big city squares, and they would be buried in the graveyard in the Acropolis. Of course, Hierapolitan athletes would attend games in other cites, and thus contact would be obtained. These contacts were shown in written reports and even on coins. Water games, animal fights and Gladiator fights were also included in the festivals.

Because of these many festivals held for Apollo, many temples were built. We obtain the information about these festivals from the coins printed in the second and third centuries A.D. Other than this information, the coins also tell us that together with the cult of Leto, the mother of Apollo and Artemis, the cult of Apollo was of great importance. Priests who attented from other cities were treated with a lot of respect. These festivals were always very joyous and exuberant.

"They'd bring their women and children
Then they'd start the games
Others would come and visit
For contests of song and dance
Watching them one would feel
They were immortal
For them there is no thing as time,
As age...

Still today, festivals are held in the part of Pamukkale where the antique theater is.

THE REMNANTS OF HIERAPOLIS

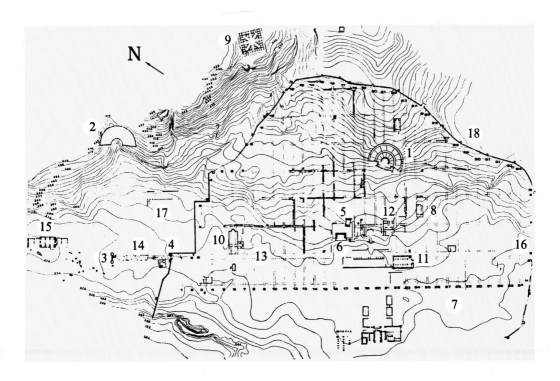

The Plan of Hierapolis

1- Theater	7- Gymnasium and its Agora	13- The road with columnes
2- Hellenistic Theater	8- Church	14- The Domitian Road
3- Frontinus (Domitian) Door	9- Martyrion of St. Philip	15- Northern Grand Bath (Basilica)
4- Southern Byzantine Door	10- Basilica	16- Southern Door
5- Apollon Temple	11- Basilica	17- Agora of commerce center
6- Monumental Fountain (Nymphaeum)	12- Southern Grand Bath	18- Defense walls of the city

The first archeological excavations were conducted by a German team, C.Humann-Jodaich-Winkler, after a research dome by C.Humann in 1887. The excavation procedures have been collected in the book called "Alte Trümer von Hierapolis" (The Old Remnants of Hierapolis). In 1957, Prof. Dr. Paola Varzone, in contact with the Italien Archeological Institute, continued with the excavations. After 1973, the same team, together with excavations, also started restorations, and today the same team is still working there.

Hierapolis is one of the antique cities which was built according to the Hippodomes "Grill Plan" on a 300x300 m

---

Southern Byzantine Door

terrace. It is made of small chambers which are made of street and roads intersecting each other to the directions East-West and North-South. Just like in Priene, some religious and large social buildings are constructed on two chambers. In this plan mathematics plays a very important part. The city has developed towards the East-West direction, and it is bisected by a 1 km long, 13.5 m wide main road from north to south.

In Hierapolis, big buildings, memorials, and commerce centers were lined alogn this road. The city was actually ornamented with flowers and trees because there was plenty of water. The plentiness of the thermal water made it possible to build public baths, and it was even possible to conduct this water into private baths of the houses. In the second and third centuries A.D. it developed a lot, and became a prosperous city. Especially during the times of Constantine, it even gained an importance because it became the key of the trade road between the East and the West. The fact that one of Christ's Apostles, St. Phillip, had lived here. It shows us that Hierapolis was still a religious center during the first years of Christianity, just as it had been in the antique times.

Being an important religious center, Hierapolis was also an important citadel. The city walls belonging to the Hellenistic period have been torn down by many earthquakes. Later, these walls have been reconstructed more strongly durgn the Roman Era. And, in the Byzantine Era, the walls have been supported against Turkish attacks. The walls in the north are surrounded by two round bastions. The road that passes through the city, continues beyond the city walls, and some parts of the wall construction are not fine, and done in a different manner. This shows us that the walls had been reconstructed.

At the verynorth, there is a gate with three sections, which looks like a victory arch because of the round bastions which are supporting the gate at each side. This gate is the last exit of the main street of Hierapolis. It has been protected very well, and there is also an inscription dedicated to Emperor Domitian. (84-85 A.D.). Because of this inscription this gate is called the Domitian Gate, or the Roman Gate. At the place where the road from the Domitian Gate to the south crosses the walls, is the Byzantine Gate. This gate outside the city walls shows us that in the earlier times the city Kydara did not have any walls.

Architectural remnants of the Apollon Temple (up)
A marble pediment cap (middle)
The museum garden. Grave stones (down)
General view of the Frontinus (Domitian) Door
(up right)
The panorama of the Byzantine Door and the
Domitian Road from the Door arches (down right)

THE BIG NORTH BATH

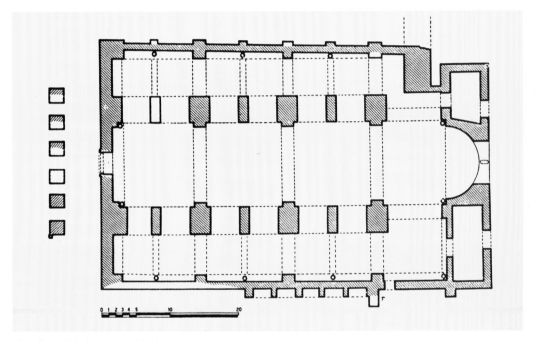

The plan of Northern Grand Bath

The healing effect of the water, which has been known for years, caused many public baths other than private baths to be built. The water did not burn the skin and once a person went in to take a bath, he would not want to come out of it again. The water was good for high blood pressure, rheumatism and arteriosclerosis.

On the north side of the Domitian Gate, which was made by the Romans, near the northern Necropolis, the bath which has preserved itself almost to its original height,

can be seen. The holes in the voults show that at those times, when it was used as a bath, these parts were filled with marbles. From the marks which still can be seen, it is obvious that the bottom of the columns covered with plaster made of lime and sand, and looked like marble. After the 19th century, this kind of mixture decreases the possibility of cracking. That is why these plasters last longer. The Big North Baths was probably converted into a church in the 5th century A.D..

Northern Grand Bath. Exterior arches ,
its large interior hall and views from the apse.

THE APOLLO TEMPLE AND NYMPHAEUM

The Apollo Cult had a strong impact on Hierapolis. And, the remnants of the Temple made for this cult (supposedly in the 3rd century A.D.) have also been found in the recent excavations. Almost none of the remnants found could be older than the 3rd century A.D. except for the remnants of the Walls around the Temple.

This might indicate that an earlier temp le might have been built in the Hellenistic ages, again for Apollo. Other than this, there also are coins which date the Apollon Cult back to the 2nd century B.C.. On one side of these coins, there is an Apollo head carrying a laurel garland.

The fountain in the Poribolos of the Temple dates back to the 2nd century A.D.. This also proves that the Temple was made sometime earlier.

On the ancient Hierapolis coins, we see that beside the Apollo Cult, the Leto Cult was celebrated as well, and festivals were held in honor of this holiness.

The measures of the Temple, of which the front walls are facing the south-west, are 20-25 m. It consists of the Pranaos and the Cella.

When we follow the main road towards the south, we reach the Nympheum which has been protected quite well. This fountain, which was made in the 2nd century A.D., has been constantly repaired until the 5th century A.D. Being a high building on the water reservoir, it is a typical Roman construction. The pieces, which can be seen today, belonging to its façades, have been found during the recent excavations. The fountain is inside the Peribolis of the Apollo Temple.

THE THEATER

Plan of the Theater

In front of the swimming pool of the Turizm Hotel and Baths, lies the columned road. The best preserved place of Hierapolis, the Theater, can be reached if this road is followed towards the south. This theater has been built by Emperor Hydrianus in the 2nd century. A.D.. The amphi (semi-circle) part faces the south. The frond side of the theater, which can take 15 to 20 thousand spectators, is 100 m long and the entrance is made of marble. 4 gates, 6 niches and 10 columns

An inscripted architrave part (at the top)
A relief with mask and Eros figure (middle left)
An embroidered marble block (middle right)
A masked block from the theater symbols (down left)
Next page:
General view of front side of the theater (up)
The marble stage door constructed in manner of the
Severius' Period (down left)
Exit doors to Cavea through the Diazoma corridors (down right)

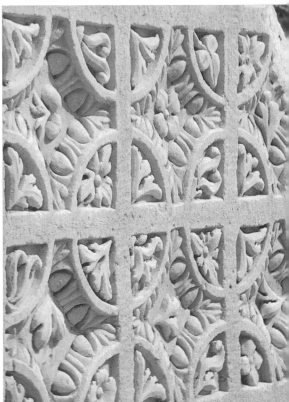

The scene of the theater and a view from the orchestra

can be seen on the ground floor. The upper floor has been destroyed by earthquakes.

The lower part of the Hierapolis theater scene is ornamented with high reliefs like the Side and Perge theaters. These high-reliefs contain legends about Apollo and Artemis. The podium is made of 60 white, high-relief marbles and the measures of these marbles are 70-90 cm. On the left side of the stage, there are high-reliefs of Artemis, and on the right side there are high-reliefs of Apollo.

THE APOLLO HIGH-RELIEFS

The first part: It is about Apollo's birth and childhood. The Hierogama of Zeus and Leto has been engraved according to classical sculpture forms. This is followed by Apollo's birth and being crowned by nymphs.

The second part: Here some myths are described. There is a description of the God's victory, who has beaten his enemy in a fight. There is a young man in the lap of a dressed women who is standing infront of a naked god, who is filling the burning Altar with Libation. This is a description of Adonis who dies in the arms of Aphrodite after being wounded by Apollo. These are followed by the War with the Gigants, and then other high-reliefs of the crowning of Apollo in the shape of Delphinos.

The thirt part: This part is dedicated to the legend of Marsyas. This legend tells about Marsyas who found the flageolet

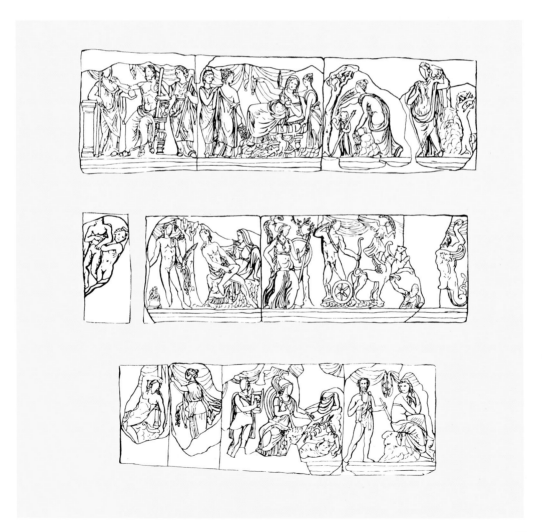

which Goddess Athena threw away because it made her look ugly while she was playing it. After starting to play the pipe, Marsyas became so fond of his voice that he even dared to compete with Apollo's lyre. They chose the Tmolos (Bozdağ) God as the arbitrator. After the first competition, none of the sides could gain superiority over the other. So, a second competiton was held. The winner of this one was Apollo, and Marsyas was punished by him. Marsyas was tied on a tree and eventually he was skinned... In this group Apollo is also being crowned.

The fourth part: Inthis part, Apollo is spinkling water from the cup in his hand onto the dancing children, as if he wants to purify himself from his sins.

The fifth part: In this part, the Muses, Klie, Eurterpe, Thalia, Melpomene, Terpsikhore, Eroto, Polhymnia, Urania and Kalliope are dancing while Apollo is playing his Cithara. The tenth Muse Sappho is holding rolls of papirus with the desire of showing her poetic art. The series ends with the Goddess Tyche high-relief.

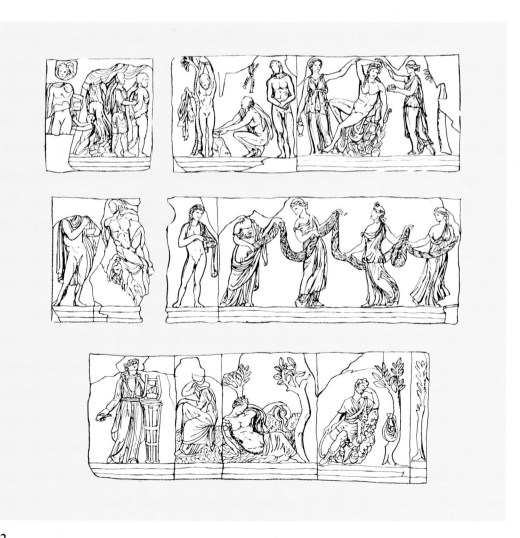

THE ARTEMIS HIGH-RELIEFS

The southern half on the high-reliefs on the podium are about Artemis legends and her Cult.

Starting at the middle of the stage, we can see the birth of Artemis and Poseidon, who is helping her. And, this is followed by the child Artemis sitting in Zeus'es lap. On the high-relief which was inspired by the "Hymn of Artemis" by Kallimachos, Leto and Athena can be seen also. In this one, Gods and women are described.

In the front part, the wild boar hunts are presented in three themes: Artemis is standing, and she is preparing for the hund; Artemis is watching the boar hunt in the cart which is being pulled by deer; Artemis is sitting beside the animals she has killed.

In the Exedra, the children of Niobe, who have been killed by Artemis and Apollo, can be seen. On the right hand side of the exedra, we can see Artemis who is proceeding with her bow and arrow. The following three high - reliefs show the dead and wounded daughters of Niobe. After the exedra door, we can see Apollo who is pointing his arrow, and then the wounded or dead children of Niobe. The last one is the one in which Niobe tries to protect her youngest son.

The forth is quite long. The cult scene about Artemis is divided into two parts: The first two high-reliefs show three children who are making incense on the goddess'es statue, and sprinkling water to help the sacrifice. In the second part we can sea a holy parade which includes many little bulls that are goind to be sacrificed. In this parade there are also two pipers. After the scene which shows Libation filled up by a priest, this series ends showing Artemis,

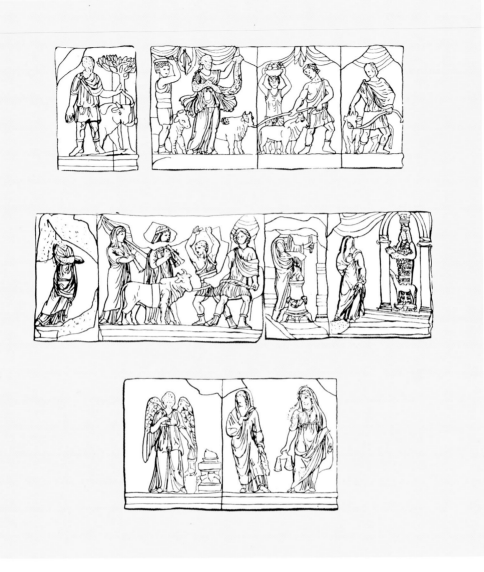

a woman praying in front of Ephesia, and three-women praying with their heads looking up.

On the last scene which is between the Cavea and the side gate, there is a high-relief showing three women. The first woman is Nemesis who is holding reins in her left hand, an is standing on the altar with her tributes. The other is Goddess Iusttita (Dike) who is holding her scales. The third one cannot be identified because her tributes cannot be seen clearly, but it is supposedly Goddess Elpis (Ümit). The presence of these three goddesses has probably something to do with the athletic games held in this part of the theater.

The recesses on the front side of the Hyposcaenium (understage). Stone ornaments belonging to the Severius Period

The Hierapolis theater gains recognition among the similar ones in Little Asia because of the sculptural ornaments, its unity and its being well protected.

We can estimate from the dedication writings of Emperor Septimius Severus that, this building was constructed in 206-208 A.D.. The inscriptions and sculptural pieces are presented in an iconographic way, and they are neatly organized to show the major analysis of the politics, religion and the cultural life of the city. The sophist Antipatros has a special place among citizens being the tutor of Geta and Caracalla, during the most developed times of the city.

The statues have a certain characteristic in their style. They are characterized together with the simple meaning of harmony, with the effects of other artistic milieus such as that of Pamphilia and Aphrodisias. An inscription found on the stage says that some parts of the sculptural ornaments are made of Dokimeion marbles, and that some of the expenses are covered by the dark-red-wool-dyers.

The usage of this Dokimeion marble also explains why there are more sculpture workshops in Phrygia in relation to other artistic centers in Little Asia.

The theater underwent some restoration in the 3rd century A.D., when the sound accord of the theater was harmed. The theater was also used in the 5th and 6th centuries A.D.. The shape of the orchestra was changed during the Roman reign.

In the middle of the Cavea (the seats made of stone) is the Emperor's box. The upper Cavea is made of 25, and the lower is made of 20 seats. These seats which have remained until today are still being used. The Hierapolis theater is being restored by a team of scientists who work for the Italian Archeological Institute.

A woman statue on the stage façade (up left)
A stage front side column crown constructed in
manner of the Severius' Period (down left)
Recesses of the front side of understage
(hyposcaneum) (right up and middle)
The marble relief showing Hierapolis
Personification (right bottom)

THE SOUTHERN BIG BATH

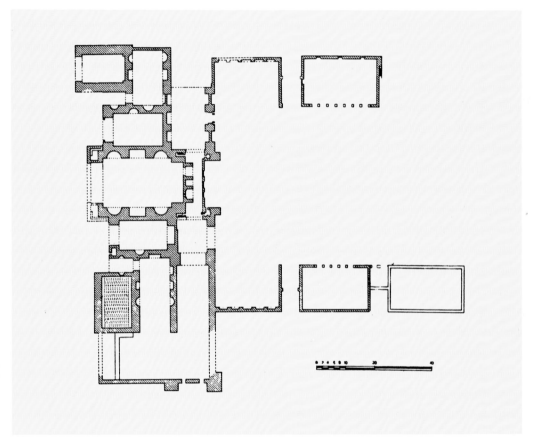

Plan of the Southern Grand Bath (Museum)

This complex which was built in the 2nd century A.D., consists of the Palestra and the bath parts. The measures of the bath, which can be entered through the Palestra, are 36x12x52 m. Through the Palestra you can go into the Frigidarium (the cold place), then the Tepidarium (the warm place) and finally the Caldarium (the hot place)

The bath is covered and vaulted. The ten rooms to the north and the south, which are next to the big hall, were reserved for the Emperors. The walls of this bath were made of marbles just like the northern

A marble relief with mask and girland (up)
Byzantine Column cap (down left) and Column examples (down right)

bath. The big halls used to lean on archs. In front of each hall there were six, four-cornered stone columns. Some of the four cornered niches in the rooms served ornamental purposes, and some were used for taking baths.

The Southern Big Bath is used today as a museum in which the pieces from excavations are exhibited.

We can see that the Hierapolis sculptures have been affected by the high style of the antique Aphrodisias.

Southern Grand Bath. One of the rooms having cradle vaultes on the ceiling.
A sarcophagus lid ornamented with women and men figures (down)

THE BASILICA

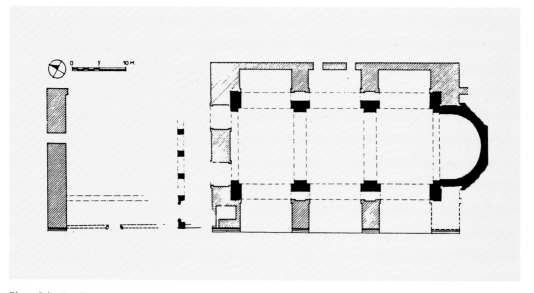

Plan of the Basilica

It is situated to the east of the Big Bath, and it is at right next to the road. It must have been built after Hierapolis became the center of Bishopry. The Basilica lies to both the south and the north. The Apsis is on the south wall. It is divided into three esplanades. Hierapolis had been a religious center since the antique times.

Before Christianity, there were many temples built for the Kybele and Leto Cult other than those built for Apollo and Artemis. There fore, the cullts of the antique Gods had their places in the city.

Hierapolis played an important role in the emergence and spread of Christianity. There fore, it became the Holy City of Little Asia. Churches started to be built in the 1st century A.D. After Christianity became the official religion, we see that Basilica type of Çhurches were made. The construction of Basilicas and Churches caused this and other Anatolian city to acquire a Roman architectural style. The big church remnants seen today show that these were built in the Antonin Era.

The big churches in Hierapolis were placed at right the main street. One of these churches is to the north of the Basilica, and on the eastern side of the main street. It has a double Apsis, one being on the short eastern wall and the other being on the southern wall. It also has six esplanades which intersect each other.

Hierapolis, which was a big religious center, was divided into 41 Bishopries.

THE AGORA

Towards the direction to the southern gate, which is close to the Gymnasium and the Big Bath, was the big bazaar place, the Agora. In this place, the bazaar used to take place, and big meetings were heldl. During the excavations some inscriptions were found in the area of the Agora. These inscriptions, eventhough little, give information about the administration, commerce and the social life of the antique times. The antique Lycos Valley has had an important part on growing cotton. And cities like Laodikia and Hierapolis were very much developed in cotton growing and weaving because of the city had improved a lot. The wool used for weaving was obtained from specially raised sheep. Being a shepperd was a favorable job. The chemical quality of the water helped Hierapolis to be developed in the art of weaving.

There were many carpet workshops and factories in the city. The main part of weaving was made of wool weaving. The necessary raw material was produced by the city. The dying, threading and weaving was done by the slaves in town.

In the city vegetal dye was used. And the carbonic water helped the dying industry a lot. The red dye was especially famous. In his book "Geography", Strabon says that the water of Hierapolis is unbelievably suibtable for wool dying. He continues that the wool dyed with roots is much more superior to the wool dyed with red (Coccus) and purple. The red dye was obtained from a plant, and this plant was raised especially for this dye. So, the famous purple (Erguvani) dye was thus improved. The plant, which made up the essence of the dye, was called Purpor. Other than floor carpets, also small carpets, woven in embroidery frames, were woven for ornamental and covering purposes.

In the city where agriculture had also developed, watering was done by the help of canals. Other than vineyards, cotton, flowers cereals, and fruits were important, too. The remnants, which today look empty and barren, were supposedly covered with green plants and flowers in the antique times.

We can also understand that, wine trade was very much developed too, from the remnants of the wine houses, and from the winejars found. Other than this, the grape squeezing pools made of marble which represent the God of Wine, Ecstasy and Love, and Dionysos, show us that, there was a cult of Dionysos, and that, wine trade was very much developed.

Today, only a few columns of the Agora remain.

A remnant from the Agora, the Syphinx figured column cap at the entrance of the Basilica (It is constructed being influenced by the Pergamon Art)

67

THE SAINT PHILLIP MARTYRIUM

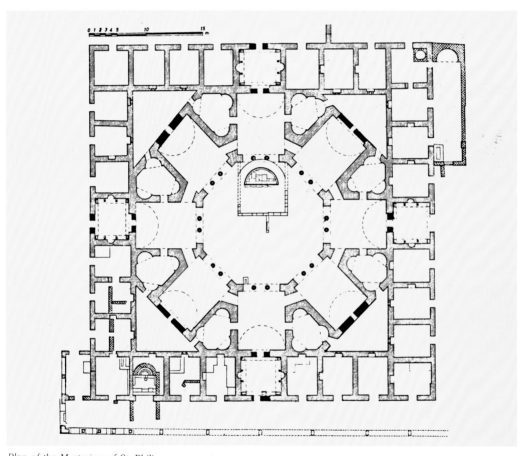

Plan of the Martyrium of St. Philip

One of the interesting buildings is the Saint Phillip Martyrium, which is located to the east of the theater, and which is outside the walls. Saint Phillip, who was one of the twelve Apostles, tried very much to spread Christianity in Hierapolis. And, together with his sons, he founded the first Christian community. He was killed in this city in 87 A.D..

This martyrium, which was made in his name as a memorial, has a square plan. Its measures are 20x20 m, and it has eight

Reconstruction of the St. Philip Martyrium

corners. In this building it is supposed that there are the tombs of Saint Phillip and his sons. But they have not been uncovered as of yet. The building was uncovered after excavations, and from the remnants the plan could be figured out. According to the plan, the building could be entered through the center, by stairs. The room, which used to be reached after the main entrance, was covered with a coppola. The big room used to lead to eight cornered, chapeled, and small rooms. Besides being rooms for praying, these rooms were at the same time residences for the pilgrims who came to visit. The ceilings of these smalls rooms must have been made of wood.

The inner part has a crucifix design, and the rooms, which are in the corners of this plan, all open up to the main room.

On the north-west side of the Martyrium, we can see the remnants of the Hellenistic period theater. Of this theater today, only some seat traces, and the hole of the cavea can be seen.

THE NECROPOLIS

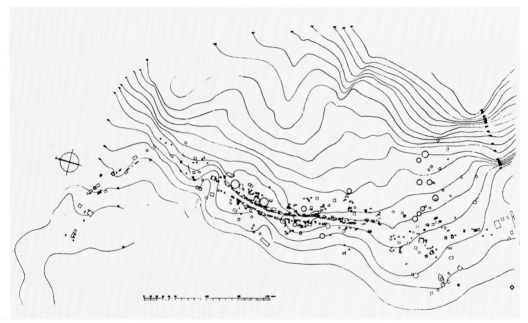

Plan of Nekropolis

Among the remnants of Hierapolis, the Necropolis has an important part. These memorial graves show us the splendid greatness of the city. The Hierapolis graves make-up on eof the biggest Necropolis in Anatolia. It comprises three parts: The southern, the northern and the eastern Necropolis. Another characteristic of these graves is that, they are seperated according to the personality of the dead. The graves of the Important People, the Heroes, and the Common People are all seperated.

The small temples called Minerva are among the graves. Some graves, of the many important people and heroes who had won athletics games in the contests, are still found in the Necropolis.

The grave types of the Hierapolis Necropolis can be divided into three parts according to the eras:

a) Tumulus
b) The Sarcophagus
c) The tombs like houses (these belong to the period between the Lake Hellenlistic Era and the Byzantine era.

A tomb construction in tumulus type (up). A tomb room with cornices on the top of the walls (down)

Monumental type graveyard with a podium on which various sarcophaguses were put

ANCIENT RUINS
IN LYCOS REGION

Laodicia: The city, which is 6 kms to the east of Denizli, near the Hisar village and between the Gümüşçay and Ellez creeks, was built in the 3rd century B.C., by the Selevkos King Antricos II., on top of the old Dyopoli city. The city was named Laodicia after his wife Laodicee. Laodicia became important because it was situated on the road which connected trade centers such as Ephesus and Miletos to Mesopotamia, and thus it was linked to Rome in the 1st century B.C.. One of the first seven churches during the sprend of Christianity was built in Laodicia.

Laodicia stayed under the reign of Byzantine, after the splitting of Rome. Later, it was taken over by Kılıç Arslan, after the Seljuks entered Anatolia. The fights between the Byzantine and the Seljuks, affected the city in a bad way, and with hthe contribution of the earthquakes the citizens began to desert the city. Some of the citizens founded, a city, known as Denizli today.

Colossaı (Honaz): Not much left is colossai which was founded on the hills 5 kms away from the south of Honaz. From the city, which had lived between the 5th century B.C. and the 8th century A.D., some traces of the Roman period theater, and again some traces of some construction foundations can be seen.

Tripolis: This antique city, which is 44 kms away from Denizli, was founded between the Big Menderes river and Yenice Village. The city which was first constructed for the purpose of defense was later reconsturcted by the Romans. We understand from the 1st century A.D. coins that, the Apollo Cult had a lot of importance in the city. We learn from resources that the city was taken by Yakupbey of the Seljuk Germiyanoğulları in the 11th century A.D.. It is also supposed that like all the other citizens of the Lycos valley, the citizens of Tripolis have deserted it because of the many earthquakes, and went to the district known as Buldan today.

Eventhough very little,, it is possible to see some remnants of the theater, the city walls, and some other buildings.

Antique theater of Laodiceia

SOME ARCHAEOLOGICAL TERMS

ABSID: Buckled salient located behind naves in the churches or basilicas.
AKROTER: Base located on top or sides of a front plate, carrying a sculpture and ornament piece.
ALKOV: A room assigned for worship alone.
ANTA: Short salient wall built on building sides, and especially in the temples.
AUDITORIUM: Place of meeting at public shows, in the ancient Greek and Roman buildings.
DIAZOMA: Horizontal passage along the seat rows in the Theatre Cavea.
EKSEDRA: Salient place or Alkov, type half circle where elevated seats are located.
EPISTYL: Name of the head-base blocks situated on the columns.
FRIEZE: Lateral section between the corniches and the head-base on the eaves.
HYPOKAUST: Underbase heating system.
CAVEA: Theater auditorium.
NAOS: Main room (Cell) where God sculptures are preserved in Greek temples.
NECCORUS: Temple assigned to the Emperor for worship and the city where this temple is located.
NYMPHAEUM: Structure ornamented with sculptures, vases and fountains, devoted to Nymphesare known as water, forest and mountain fairies in ancient Greek literature.
ODEION: Small structure like a theatre, employed for recitals and dramas.
PALASTRA: Open courtyard employed for athletics.
PERYDOLOS: Surrounding wall around the temple walls.
PODIUM: Smooth, sound base situated under structures or structure elements.
PORTIC: Open corridor covered by a roof and ending with columns.
PRONAOS: Front room in the temples, facing west in general.
PROPYLON: Monumental structure located on front of palaces, temples or cities in the ancient Greek civilizations.
SELLA: Main room where the worship sculpture is located in the temples.
SKENE: Scene of the ancient Greek theatres.
STYLOBAT: Stone basis situated under a column row.
STOA: Column row covered with a roof.
TETRASTOON: A rectangular area surrounded by four stoas or column rows.

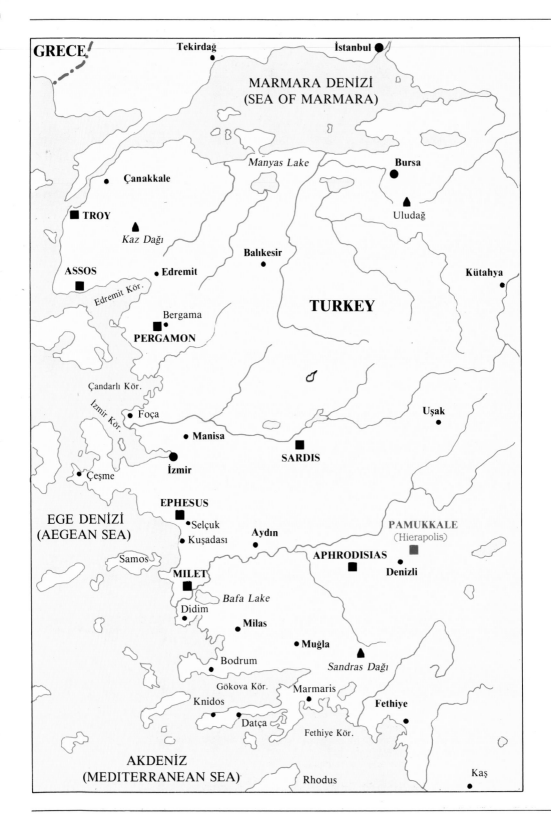

BIBLIOGRAPHY

- Carl Humann, Conrad Cichorius, Walther Yodeich Franz Winter: Altertumer Von Hierapolis – Berlin-1898

- E.AKURGAL: Ancient Civilazations and Ruins of Turkey – İstanbul-1978

- A.ERHAT : Mitoloji Sözlüğü – İstanbul - 1978

- M.ÖZSAİT: Hellenistik ve Roma Devrinde Pisidya Tarihi İstanbul-1985

- Z.TAŞLIKLIOĞLU: Anadolu'da Apollon Kültü ve İlgili Kaynaklar – İstanbul-1963

- R.TULLIA & D'A. FRANCESCO: Le Sculture del Teotro Iricevi con Cicli di Apolle e Artemide – Roma-1985

- P.AYDEMİR: Aynı Eser (Özel Tercüme)

- İ.AKŞİT: Anadolu Uygarlıkları – İstanbul-1982

- İ.PARMAKSIZOĞLU: İBNİ BATUTA Seyahatnamesi'nden Seçmeler – İstanbul-1971

- D.HASOL: Ansiklopedik Mimarlık Sözlüğü – İstanbul-1979

- A.MUFİT MANSEL: Ege ve Yunan Tarihi – Ankara-1971

- M.ÖKMEN: Herodot Tarihi – İstanbul-1973

- T.TOKER: Pamukkale

- F.AKKAKOCA: Pamukkale Suları